"WISE AND HUMOROUS. . . . A SENSE OF TIME-LESSNESS PERVADES THIS DELICATE AND FINELY TUNED BOOK."

Publishers Weekly

"Jacob is a most appealing, most refreshing character, entirely believable when he answers the questions with simple practical, sometimes even metaphysical wisdom."

William Griffin
Religion Editor
Publishers Weekly

"[Jacob] is a good man. . . . Many of the little dialogues have a Zen-like charm."

Clifton Fadiman

"Communicates some profound truths in a pithy, gentle manner and the overall impression the text makes on the reader is that it was authored by a wise, generous spirit."

Dr. David Lieber
President of the University of Judaism

"It is an event when one comes in contact with an original mind like Noah benShea's. It is a cause to celebrate when from that mind pours forth wisdom like *Jacob the Baker*. Noah benShea's vision is at times subtle, at times dazzling. And always, he does the miraculous—he makes you smile."

Lawrence Grobel
Contributing editor of *Redbook*

"A terse, valuable series of observations. . . . I enjoyed it."

James Michener

JACOB
the
BAKER

NOAH benSHEA

Ballantine Books • New York

Library of Congress Catalog Card Number: 89-91490

ISBN: 0-345-36662-X

This edition published by arrangement with Villard Books, a division of Random House, Inc., New York.

Cover design by William Geller

Manufactured in the United States of America

First Ballantine Books Edition: June 1990

20 19 18 17 16 15

For my father
For my mother
For my children

THANK YOU

Aron Hirt-Manheimer

Danyel benShea

CONTENTS

CONTENTS

Contents

CONTENTS

CONTENTS

Then the LORD put forth His hand, and touched my mouth; and the LORD said unto me: Behold, I have put My words in your mouth. . . .

JEREMIAH 1:9

JACOB
the
BAKER

ONE MAN TRAVELING OPPOSITE THE FLOW IS MORE CLEARLY NOTICED THAN ALL WHO TRAVEL TOGETHER

*I*T was still dark when Jacob woke. He shut his eyes, pulled the covers over his head, and thanked God for returning his soul.

It was cold in his room, and the cold interfered with his ability to focus on his prayers. He knew he was saying them quickly. He prayed for understanding.

He turned on the small heater in his bathroom and dressed in front of it. The warmth soothed the back of his legs.

In the kitchen, he sliced a piece of hard cheese and dark bread. He ate slowly while the tea water boiled. When the tea was ready, Jacob clenched a cube of sugar between his teeth and relished in the hot tea, sliding slowly past the sweetness.

"Surely," he thought to himself, "this is a taste of life in the world to come."

The moon was still high as he walked to the bakery. His boots crunched the snow, and the sound traveled back to his youth. He felt a great truth between the silver moon, the white snow, and the black night.

The shutters on most of the homes remained closed, their worlds asleep. He remembered a time when an old man would rap on the shutters and call people to morning prayers.

The old man was gone. He wondered what people would do if he started banging on their shutters.

He hurried on.

Behind the bakery, pigeons pecked circles in the hard ground, finishing the crumbs from yesterday's bread.

Jacob stared at the tracks the birds left in the shallow pockets of snow. The three-fingered pattern radiating out of a single source . . . the patriarchs: Abraham, Isaac, and Jacob . . . the past, the present, and the future . . . "Yes," thought Jacob, "it fits. It all fits."

The pigeons rose and settled on the rain gutters.

Jacob stood by himself, staring up at the stars between the buildings that pressed in on him.

He looked at his hands as he unlocked the rear door of the factory. Then he stepped from the night into the reassuring blackness of the bakery. "It is like pulling a prayer shawl over my head," he thought. "This darkness is my own."

He was stiff. Bending to fire the oven was an effort. From his knees, he hypnotically watched the pilot light and sensed its affirmation. He thought of the "eternal light" and patience. He prayed for such patience.

This was the oldest bakery in his community, and, though much had changed, the original oven remained. The bread it baked rode 'round and 'round on a ferris wheel of shelves. Jacob paused and laid his cheek on the warming bricks outside the old oven.

Soon the oven would reach temperature. Soon the other bakers would arrive. They could sleep later in the morning, see their children before they left for school. Jacob lived alone.

He was not lonely. He was cut from life but not removed.

He turned on the mixer and began to work the first dough. His eyes followed the spiral metal arm on its endless roll. Its pattern confirmed a truth he saw everywhere.

Gradually, he added the warm water, careful not to make the dough too stiff or too wet. Moderation. Balance. Taking measure of what he was doing.

Jacob the baker understood this.

Now there was time. His time. A little time. The dough needed to rise. The oven's heat curled through the bakery.

Jacob took a thick flat pencil from his back pocket and began to write. But, it really wasn't Jacob writing.

Jacob was a reed, and the breath of God blew through Jacob, made music of him.

In this way, was Jacob's voice.

Jacob finished just as the other bakers arrived. He folded the little pieces of paper with his scratchings and shoved them under the scale on the dough bench. At the end of the day, he would collect his thoughts and add them to the stacks at home. Now, he would make bread.

Cold air and light broke in through the back door. The bakery filled with activity. Men were coming and going with large silver pans of braided egg loaves, frosting white cakes with castles and pride, building biscuits, rolls, and bagels into tottering towers which collapsed into baskets where customers could, with delicious anticipation, pick their favorites.

Clearly, Jacob was a man on his path in the process of this work. He did not appear to be laboring. He was at one with his efforts. He knew what another baker needed without being asked. When Jacob worked with others, doors sprung open just when a load became unbearable and closed behind men who often forgot to do so. In this way, Jacob's contribution wasn't simply the addition of another person's efforts. It was, rather, that with Jacob one and one made three. He made the others more than they might have been. He didn't think it made him more. He didn't think about this at all.

Work for Jacob was, in many ways, like a prayer. It was a repetition, leading him out of himself and up Mt. Sinai with the grace of a soul not restrained by the weight of its own importance.

"Jacob!" a voice shouted, cutting through the bakery.

It was Samuel, the owner. He called for Jacob from the half-open swinging door that divided the bakery from the store.

Samuel was approximately the same age as Jacob but round and almost bald. And, like the few people who actually knew Jacob, Samuel treated Jacob in a special way.

Jacob didn't demand such consideration. It was just that Jacob couldn't be treated like the others. Having Jacob work for him, somehow, made Samuel feel like a more religious man.

"Jacob," asked Samuel, "how are you?"

Jacob didn't say anything but simply angled his head to one side, knowing the question had nothing to do with why he had been called.

And Samuel knew that Jacob knew. And, in that moment, such was the wonderful silence both men shared.

"Jacob, I have a customer with a special request, but I need your help."

Jacob smiled.

Samuel raised his eyebrows, offered a helpless grin, and continued. "Jacob, you know all those little pieces of paper you've been writing on for years with your ideas, or thoughts, or whatever you call them?"

"I don't call them anything," said Jacob.

"It's not what you call them that's important," said Samuel, now holding his palms upward like a man frustrated trying to catch rain.

"Somehow, one of your 'ideas' found its way into a customer's loaf of bread, and this lady thinks I put it there on purpose. Now she wants me to sell her bread for a community dinner, but each of the loaves must have one of your thoughts in it."

Samuel's face began to plead. "So? What do you say? Will you do it?"

Jacob pulled on his lower lip with his thumb and forefinger. "What was written on the piece of paper in her bread?"

"I don't know," said Samuel. "Why don't you ask the lady? She wants to meet you. Come up front!"

Like a reluctant character dragged before the footlights on a giant stage, Jacob grew shy when he came into the retail section of the bakery.

Waiting there was a dark-haired lady, holding gloves in one hand and a purse in the other. She shifted her purse to the same hand that held her gloves so she could reach out and greet Jacob.

When she released his hand, she continued to stare down at the flour dust settling on the floor where Jacob stood. She swallowed in an attempt to gather herself.

"Did you write this?" she asked, thrusting one of Jacob's notes forward.

The note read: *"Wisdom does not make me full. It fills me with hunger."*

Jacob looked at the paper and nodded his head.

"How wise you must be," said the lady, with great flattery. "All my life I've been pursuing wisdom, and you've captured my frustration. I feel like a fool."

"Anyone who has struggled with wisdom has felt like a fool," said Jacob.

The lady and Samuel stood there in silence, looking at Jacob and weighing his remark.

Then, they looked back and forth at each other, then back at Jacob, then back at each other.

"Well, will he do it?" she asked Samuel, as if Jacob weren't there.

Samuel turned to Jacob. "Well, will you do it? Will you let us have some of your ideas for the bread?"

Jacob grinned. "Only arrogance guards what it doesn't own!"

Samuel nodded to the lady. "He'll do it."

The lady returned her focus to Jacob. "Thank you," she said.

But Jacob had already retreated to the bakery, leaving her appreciation to find peace on the ground where Jacob left his footprints, in the flour dust.

Jacob traced his path to work on the way home. He traveled within. A small, frozen puddle of water, caught by a rock, huddled next to a curb and drew his attention.

"An eternity is any moment opened with patience," he reminded himself.

Then he raised the tip of his boot and pushed down on the layers of ice. He could feel the pressure of the lady's request that morning in the bakery.

The ice cracked under the insistence of his boot, sending a map of new patterns across the surface.

He continued home and noted spring was in the air.

Jacob warmed a cup of soup for dinner and finished the heel of his morning bread.

His books of learning surrounded him, their blue binding appearing black in the light.

Small pads of yellow paper, a stack of blank white paper, pencils, and pens crowded a worn wooden desk.

Jacob sat to write but did not. The clean innocence of the empty pages instead invited his imagination on an ancient route, and, on that journey, absent of eternal arguments of logic and reason and individual perspective, Jacob climbed his ladder.

During the night, angels stared down through the stars into Jacob's world. They watched him sleep. They commented on the way his body folded on the bed. They liked this man. They drew their wings over him and stood guard by his soul.

The next morning, Samuel's voice flexed with excitement as it again reached into the bakery and begged for Jacob's attention.

"That lady is back," shouted Samuel. "Everyone loved your 'thoughts' in their bread. But, they want more. They all want more. Will you do it for me?"

Max, the young man with thick muscles, who carried the flour sacks, gave Jacob a gentle elbow in the ribs and winked at him.

"How much will they pay you? Maybe you can make some extra money, eh?" Max raised his voice at the end of his sentence.

"You know, he may be right," said Samuel. "Are you interested, Jacob?"

"No!" said Jacob with amusement. "Greed only uses expectation to arrive at despair."

Max was intrigued. "Does that mean you're going to give them your thoughts for nothing?"

"I will," said Jacob, touched by Max's form of caring.

Jacob nodded his consent to Samuel.

"Thank you," said Samuel, and he meant it. But, from somewhere, in an unarticulated voice, he knew his friend's life was changing. Forever.

And Samuel was right. Because now, people hurried to the bakery, anxious to ask Jacob how they should live, and what should be said to this child, and how do I struggle with this sadness?

They came in haste and noise and deep concern. They reached out to touch him as he walked down the street.

The secret of Jacob became a whisper, which rode the wind into every ear, and the community embraced Jacob as if he were a long-ignored human treasure suddenly unearthed.

TRUTH,
MIRACLES,
AND MORE

"*T*ELL us the truth about life!" someone asked Jacob.

And Jacob responded. "Language is only a lie told about the truth."

"Can you show us a miracle, Jacob?" they asked.

And he answered. "A miracle is often the willingness to see the common in an uncommon way."

"How can we have more, Jacob?"

And Jacob answered. "The only way I can take a breath is by releasing my breath. In order to be more, I must be willing to be less."

THE REASON
FOR RELIGION
IS NOT REASON

A student, clearly troubled by something Jacob had said, followed him as he left the bakery.

"Jacob, did you say that what is holy has no beginning or end?"

"Yes."

"But that is not possible," said the student.

"That is because only the possible can be measured," said Jacob.

The student struggled to understand. "Jacob, you are not making sense."

Jacob nodded in agreement, then placed his hands in front of the student, covering her eyes.

"You see," said Jacob, "reason explains the darkness, but it is not a light."

BUILDING FEAR

A community leader came to see Jacob, hoping to find peace of mind, an ease for his burden.

The man was troubled by a repetitive dream that he did not understand.

"Jacob, in my dream, I have traveled a long distance and am finally arriving at a great city. But, at the entrance to the city, I am met by a tall soldier who says that I must answer two questions before I am admitted. Will you help me?"

Jacob nodded.

"The first question the soldier asks is 'What supports the walls of a city?' "

"That is easy," said Jacob. "Fear supports the walls of a city."

"But what supports the fear?" asked the man. "For that is the second question."

"The walls," answered Jacob. "The fears we cannot climb become our walls."

IT IS ALREADY GROWING LIGHT

A neighbor of Jacob's needed to start on a journey, but it was the middle of the night.

Afraid to begin, afraid not to begin . . . he came to Jacob.

"There is no light on the path," he complained.

"Take someone with you," counseled Jacob.

"Jacob, what do you mean? If I do that, there will be two blind men."

"You are wrong," said Jacob. "If two people discover each other's blindness, it is already growing light!"

AN ETERNITY
IS ANY MOMENT
OPENED
WITH PATIENCE

A mother and father came to Jacob and asked to speak with him about patience.

"Tell us what we need to know in order to be more patient."

"Go away," said Jacob. "I have no time for you!"

"Well," said the couple, "how do you think that makes us feel?"

"Ah," said Jacob, smiling. "That is the first lesson in learning how to be patient with others."

RIGHT AND WRONG

*T*wo men approached Jacob and asked him to decide which of them was wise.

"I know what is right," said the first man.

"I know what is wrong," said the other.

"Good," said Jacob. "Together you make one wise man."

ANGER
CANNOT BE PEELED
WITH ANGER

A middle-aged man contorted his face and waved a message of Jacob's that the man had found in a loaf of bread.

"What do you mean by this?" he asked, and he proceeded to read, *"The fist starves the hand."*

Jacob took all of the man's anger, consumed its force, and transformed it, returning peace in his voice and manner.

"When our hand is made into a fist, we cannot receive the gifts of life from ourselves, our friends, or our God.

"When our hand is closed in a fist, we cannot hold anything but our bitterness. When we do this, we starve our stomachs and our souls. Our anger brings a famine on ourselves."

The man was quiet. Those around him whispered back and forth what the man had said and what Jacob had answered. They urged the man to move on. But, Jacob wasn't done.

"Put down this fury," Jacob's eyes pleaded. "Anger locks a man in his own house."

THE ARROGANCE OF
IGNORANCE

*A*T the end of the school day, the children came and sat on the flour sacks. Jacob would sit across from the children, and they would talk.

As Jacob told his stories, he would from time to time shut his eyes. It was as if he were remembering what to say, not by searching through his mind, but by remembering what he saw. Somewhere, he had a perfect picture, and the words he spoke were a description of this vision.

"What do you see when you shut your eyes, Jacob?" asked a little girl.

"Well," Jacob said, "once upon a time there was a man who had a vision and began pursuing it.

"Two others saw that the first man had a vision and began following him.

"In time, the children of those who followed asked their parents to describe what they saw.

"But what their parents described appeared to be the coattails of the man in front of them.

"When the children heard this, they turned from their parents' vision, saying it was not worthy of pursuit."

Jacob leaned toward the little girl who had asked the question.

"So, what do we discover from this story?"

The children were quiet.

"I'll tell you," said Jacob.

"We discover children who deny what they have never experienced.

"We discover parents who believe in what they have never experienced.

"And, from this, we discover the question is not 'What do I see when I shut my eyes' but 'What do you see when you open yours?' "

IT IS ONLY A FOOL
WHO HAS NEVER FELT
LIKE ONE

"W<small>HEN</small> I shut my eyes," one of the boys snickered, "I don't see anything."

"What you see is your ignorance," said Jacob, turning his head toward the child. "And when we cannot find our ignorance, you can be sure we have lost our wisdom."

The boy's sarcasm dissolved into innocence. "I was making a joke," he said, "and now I think you're laughing at me."

"Let me tell you a story," said Jacob, his voice calming the boy as the story began.

"Once there was a fool who set out for the king's palace. Along the way, people pointed and jeered at the fool. 'Why should a man like you be going to see the king?' they laughed.

" 'Well, I'm going to be the king's teacher,' answered the fool with great assurance. But his conviction only brought even greater laughter from the people along the path.

"When the fool arrived at the palace, the king thought he would make short work and great jest of this man. So, the king had the fool immediately brought to the royal court.

" 'Why do you dare to disturb the king?' demanded His Majesty.

" 'I come to be the royal teacher,' said the fool in a very matter-of-fact manner.

"The king twisted with laughter. 'How can you, a fool, teach me?'

" 'You see,' said the fool, 'already you ask me questions.'

"The court froze silent. The king gathered himself and stared at his ridiculous opponent. 'You have offered me a clever response, but you have not answered my questions!'

" 'Only a fool has all the answers,' came the reply, balanced on a shy smile.

" 'But, but,' now the king was sputtering, 'but what would others say if they knew the king had a fool for a teacher?'

" 'Better to have a fool for a teacher than a fool for a king,' said the fool.

"When he heard this, the king, who was not a bad man, confessed, 'Now, I do feel like a fool.'

" 'No,' said the man across from him, 'it is only a fool who has never felt like one.' "

The children laughed, and Jacob felt as if he were standing in front of the little heater in his home.

PRAYER IS A PATH
WHERE THERE IS NONE

A child was filled with a question, which like an itch demanded to be scratched.

"Jacob, what I don't understand is how you are to decide whether to follow what you feel is right or what you think is right?"

Jacob touched his own chest and said, "My heart knows what my mind only thinks it knows."

The answer pushed the boy to another question.

"What if neither my heart nor mind can help me find the way?"

And Jacob answered, "Prayer is a path where there is none."

FRIENDSHIP

*A*N old friend of Jacob's was accused of a minor crime and came to see him seeking a favor.

"Jacob, I want you for my judge."

"But I want you for my friend," said Jacob.

"Can't you be both?"

"Look," said Jacob. "That judgment I have made, and already you argue with me."

WHY NOT YOU?

A man wandered for many years, searching for happiness. Much came into his possession, but no joy remained.

He came to Jacob and stood weeping, complaining about how he had been cheated in life.

Eventually, he turned his head toward Jacob and moaned, "Why me? Why me?"

And Jacob answered, "Why not you? You've looked everywhere else."

IT IS THE SILENCE
BETWEEN THE NOTES
THAT MAKES THE MUSIC

O NE evening, in the late quiet of the bakery, Jacob stood next to a stack of bread boards freshly powdered with dry cornmeal. He touched his right forefinger to his lips and then with the same finger began drawing a repetitive image in the cornmeal.

Jacob was drawing the Hebrew letter *alef*, the silent, first letter in the alphabet.

His finger moved absently, stroking the downward open line at the backbone of the sacred form.

He drew row upon row, transforming the blank bread board into a Hebraic mandala, a staircase for his soul.

Focusing on the pattern opened what was closed, and the absent sound of the silent *alef* beckoned him, drew him in.

Then, without warning, the lights went on in the other end of the bakery. It was Samuel, and he was startled to find someone still there.

"Is that you, Jacob? Are you all right?" There was real concern in Samuel's voice.

Jacob took a breath but said nothing.

"Did I interrupt you?"

Jacob chose kindness over honesty. "No," he said softly.

Samuel's focus caught on the design Jacob had marked in the cornmeal. Samuel was perplexed.

"Jacob, why do you draw this letter *alef* over and over again?"

"Because," said Jacob, "it is the silence between the notes that makes the music; it is the space between the bars that holds the tiger."

But while Jacob spoke, he knew Samuel was only half-listening, distracted by the burden of another question.

"Jacob," Samuel began and then hesitated, cautious, unsure of himself, "many people would like to spend more time with you, but they are afraid their questions bother you."

Samuel looked up to see how what he was saying was being taken.

After being invisible for most of his life, Jacob found it strange that these same people would now be concerned about disturbing him.

The history of a hidden, quiet life had served Jacob well and now lent him the strength to be—and be in public.

"Sometimes my questions bother me," Jacob said to Samuel.

"Then you don't mind?" Samuel's question was clearly phrased with hopeful expectation.

"I am happy I have been ignored until now," said Jacob, conscious of the challenge to find joy in the obligations of fate.

"Well," Samuel continued to press "then you will still put up with our questions?"

Jacob pulled his hands together in the shape of a small bowl. "Samuel, our life is a vessel, and a vessel is formed for two functions. One is to hold"—then Jacob flattened his hands as if he were making an offering,—"and the other is to pour."

Samuel understood. He backed out of the bakery. Jacob remained.

When the silence was renewed, Jacob swept his hand across the bread boards, like a tide's wash, erasing the patterns in the corn-meal.

WHEN I CAN'T FIND
MY IGNORANCE
I HAVE LOST
MY WISDOM

*J*ACOB was wakened before dawn by thunder. A dark rain danced on his roof. He wrapped himself in the weather and his prayers.

The thunder crashed again. He touched memories of his mother telling him not to fear the rumbling, telling him that it was only God moving furniture.

Jacob wondered what was being rearranged on this morning.

He bent his body into the rain and toward the bakery.

Lightning fractured the sky, then retreated to the blackness.

A student was waiting in the rain to seek Jacob's advice. The boy ran along side of Jacob and matched his stride.

"Jacob, what are the limits of a man?"

"Ask the man!" said Jacob, without losing his pace.

"And what if the man acknowledges no limits?"

"Then you've discovered his."

"But," the student persisted, "what then is the route to wisdom?"

"Humility!" came the reply.

"How long is the route?"

And Jacob answered, "I don't know.

LOSING YOURSELF

*A*T the back of the bakery, a young man leaned against the loading dock. He bit on his lower lip nervously while he spoke with Jacob.

"I'm sorry to take your time, but I'm about to be married, and . . ." The perspective groom stammered to a stop.

Jacob nodded but said nothing.

The young man began again to unfold his fear.

"I'm about to be married, but I'm afraid if I join with a woman, I will somehow lose part of myself."

Jacob moved his hand in such a way as to imply he was brushing away the fears. "Don't worry about this. If you join with a woman, you will not lose part of yourself. In fact"—Jacob patted the young man's chest—"if you join with a woman, there is a very good chance you will no longer be lost in yourself."

HEAR O ISRAEL

THROUGHOUT the day, long lines stretched into the bakery, hoping to make contact with Jacob. Jacob, for his part, didn't seem sure what to make of this attention. In fact, he didn't seem interested in making anything of it.

A man, whose facial muscles jumped as he spoke, pushed toward Jacob and in a nervous half-whisper said:

"Jacob! I keep hearing a voice calling out my name."

"But why does this make you uncomfortable?" asked Jacob.

"Because it is my voice," said the man.

Jacob took the man's hands and pressed them between his own.

"We should only be frightened when we cannot hear ourselves.

"Often we create our own deafness and then grow so familiar with our deafness that the thought of hearing becomes frightening."

A MAN WITH A LANTERN
GOES IN SEARCH
OF A LIGHT

*A*N old man was bitter and challenged Jacob with a complaint.

"All my life I have searched for meaning," he said.

"The meaning is in the search," said Jacob, waving off the man's distress.

"Then I will never find the meaning?"

"No," said Jacob. "You will never stop looking."

Jacob held his voice for a moment, unsure if he had been too harsh.

"My friend," Jacob began again, "know that you are a man with a lantern who goes in search of a light."

A FISH CANNOT
DESCRIBE WATER
UNTIL IT IS CAUGHT

A man who considered himself enlightened came to see Jacob. The man hoped to cast his shadow over Jacob's reputation.

"I'm never wrong," the man boasted.

"Ignorance is its own justice," said Jacob.

"What do you mean?" asked the man.

"My ignorance extinguishes my doubt," answered Jacob humbly.

"What does that mean?" asked the man, now clearly unsure of himself.

"It means," said Jacob, "my blindness is often reassured by what I don't know."

A PASSING TRUTH

*A*N attractive man and woman came to Jacob and asked if he could explain "beauty" to them.

"No," said Jacob; he could not.

"But isn't beauty truth? That's what the poet says."

Jacob said nothing and his silence made the couple uncomfortable.

"Why won't you answer us?" they pressed him.

"Because," said Jacob, "I'm waiting for you to become old. Then you will understand the nature of beauty and the truth of time."

I'M NOT LOST
IN A DREAM;
I'M DREAMING
I'M LOST

A very old woman, rolling her hands over and over as if they were polishing each other, began talking with Jacob but kept looking across her shoulder to see if those around her were listening.

The crowd sensed this and, out of respect for her age, moved back. Satisfied with this subtle shift in privacy, she moved even closer to Jacob and began:

"Listen, young man!" Jacob smiled at the thought. "I want to ask you something. I heard you talk about dying, and I'm going to die soon. I have a great deal of money. If you're so smart, why not tell me how I can take it with me?" The old woman released a wicked little gurgle of greed.

Jacob just looked at her.

The voice was now more raspy with impatience. "Well? Well? What can be carried to the other side?"

"Everything of value," answered Jacob, as if this insight was common knowledge.

Her greed excited, the old woman shouted, "How? How?"

Jacob drew calmer. "In your memory," he answered.

"Memory?" said the woman, dumbstruck at this suggestion. "Memory can't carry wealth!"

Jacob's focus seized the woman's eye. "That is only because you have already forgotten what is of value."

A DOOR IS A HOLE
WE CUT IN OUR WALL

A man who appeared to be a mason from the crusts of dried cement on his shirt waited patiently one day for a chance to speak with Jacob. The man's voice was gruff—but not his manner.

"Jacob, all my life I have made homes for others. Now I am preparing to build a home for myself. Do you have any suggestions?"

Jacob laughed. "Who is Jacob the baker to mix mortar and make bricks?"

But, then, Jacob raised his left index finger, as if touching an old memory, and waved it in the air, suggesting there was maybe one thought he could offer.

"It says in our books: In order for a house to be a house, it must have a window and a door."

A smile climbed the man's face. "Jacob, this much even I know." Those behind the man chuckled as well.

"But," Jacob continued, as if he did not hear their laughter, "do you know why I think a house must have a window and a door?"

Suddenly, it became very quiet again. Humility held over the crowd. People craned their necks to hear. And Jacob began again.

"My house must have a door so I can enter myself, and a window so I can see beyond myself!"

"And if it doesn't?" asked the man.

A great sadness rolled its shadow across Jacob. The words came slowly.

"We must remember," said Jacob, "the only difference between a house and a coffin is a door."

HUMILITY
IS THE INTEGRITY
OF WISDOM

WHEN the world went back to their homes, Jacob turned off the lights in the bakery and pulled the door shut behind him.

The morning rain had given way to a deep fog. For the first time since waking, he was alone.

He purposely ignored brushing off the flour that spotted his pants. It reminded him that he was a baker.

He crossed a small bridge, directing himself toward the home of an elderly man who was ill.

Jacob knocked on the door. The smell of medicines and old age waited in the air. There was no answer. He let himself in.

Mr. Gold's cane hung on the back of the door-knob. When Jacob entered, the cane began to swing like a metronome keeping time on an ancient clock.

Mr. Gold sat propped up against several pillows. Licking his forefinger, he turned the page of his Bible.

"Ah, Jacob," said Mr. Gold, his voice filled with the tone of a man slipping into something comfortable. "You come to visit me because I am sick and that is your responsibility?"

"No, Mr. Gold," said Jacob. "Your illness I visit out of responsibility. You I visit out of love."

Mr. Gold laughed, triggered by the warmth beneath Jacob's humor.

"Jacob, I hear many others are discovering how clever you are. Do you offer these people answers?"

"Hopefully I offer them a mirror."

"Don't be so humble! I wish I had your wisdom."

"No you don't!" said Jacob emphatically.

Mr. Gold leaned forward. "How do you know what I want?"

"How do you know what I know?" smiled Jacob.

THE MOMENTS
THAT THE WORLD
IGNORED
FILLED HIS PLATE

*I*T was always the small, solitary acts of living that brought Jacob peace.

The more attention others drew to him, the more pleasure he began to draw from the commonplace. The moments that the world ignored filled his plate.

He did not seem susceptible to his own inflation. On the contrary, he appeared to relish and grow more comfortable with making himself less. In this process, the subtleties of living grew, their significance enhanced.

The teapot whistled when it was ready. From this, Jacob took that he must be patient until he is called. And when he is called, he must be able to hear the call; and for this to happen he must be willing to pay attention. And when the call came, and he was listening, he must be prepared to act. Patience, calm, attention, and action—these were Jacob's thoughts in the small kitchen over his morning tea.

When he finished, the circle of the empty cup stared back at him, its rim running endlessly.

Jacob drifted, cradled himself into the silent center space of the cup and found peace.

JACOB'S RIDDLE

O NE night, while he slept, Jacob's mind stepped onto Jacob's ladder and posed a riddle.

"To what heights can a person aspire?" he asked himself.

"To the Number ONE," he heard himself answer.

"And after that?"

"And after that, Moses came down the mountain knowing less than ONE would leave the world with nothing, and more would leave the world in pieces."

WE CAN'T HEAR
WHAT'S BEING SAID
WHEN OUR FINGERS
ARE IN OUR EARS

*T*HERE was a terrible banging on Jacob's front door. From the intensity of the hammering and shouts, it became clear to Jacob he had been unaware of the noise for some time. This awareness did not disturb him. He appeared rather to enjoy it.

When the door was opened, a man with a puffy red face shouted at Jacob, "What were you doing?" Two others stood behind the inquisitor.

"Thinking," said Jacob, giving very little notice to the man's anger.

"Thinking?" repeated the man as if he were measuring Jacob's sanity.

"Yes," said Jacob, who now closed the door behind him and headed off to work.

The three agitated, middle-aged men stood blankly facing each other, and then, determined not to be left behind, they began after him.

Moments later, Jacob stopped without warning and then, to himself as much as to them, answered the question they had asked earlier.

"I was thinking about how many doors there are and how seldom we use them."

Then, again, he set off.

In order to catch up and talk with Jacob face to face, the men had to increase their pace to almost a run. When they did approach him, they were too out of breath to speak.

Jacob stopped and waited.

"Thank you," said the men, half-bent over, their hands on their hips.

When the men captured their breath, they also revived their anger. The leader tried to bring all his authority to bear in his voice.

"Look Jacob! I've seen you for a long time. You're just Jacob the baker. Now everyone wants to ask you questions, and the children come to learn from you. What do you tell them?"

Jacob was missing the warmth of the huge bakery oven. The sunrise was painting orange cracks in the gray sky.

He searched his mind for a door these men might pass through and then spoke.

"I will be glad to tell you what I have been teaching the children," he began, "but first you must all agree to put your fingers in your ears."

The men did as they were told and stood as a jury directly opposite Jacob who again began speaking.

After a few minutes, the men waved and shouted, trying to draw Jacob's attention.

"Jacob," they said, "we can't hear what's being said when our fingers are in our ears!"

"That," answered Jacob, "is what I have been telling your children."

UNDERSTANDING
ISN'T WISDOM
BUT HOW WISDOM
IS OPENED

A rich man came to Jacob and sought his advice.

"Why must I give to the poor?"

"Because they are responsible for your freedom," said Jacob.

The man was astonished. "How does giving to the poor bring about my freedom?"

"You see," said Jacob, "either the key to a man's wallet is in his heart, or the key to a man's heart is in his wallet. So, until you express your charity, you are locked inside your greed."

CHARITY
IS WEALTH'S
HIGHEST REWARD

*T*HERE was a wealthy man who only contributed to charity with great reluctance.

The poor in the community prepared to take the man to court and charge him with theft.

On a brittle cold morning, the man confronted Jacob.

"What have I stolen?" he asked, his voice shaking.

"The dignity of the poor," said Jacob.

"How did I steal the dignity of the poor?"

And Jacob answered. "By giving only to the beggar."

FREEDOM
IS NOT THE ABSENCE
OF SLAVERY;
IT IS THE MEMORY

SAMUEL stood patiently in the morning shadows of the bakery waiting for Jacob and wanting to talk.

As soon as Jacob entered, Samuel came to life, and the two men worked together, quickly finishing the tasks in waking a bakery after its rest.

"I miss these times," admitted Samuel. "I'm not sure I didn't like it better before people discovered your wisdom."

"The wisdom isn't mine," said Jacob, hunching his shoulders as if he were retreating from the very thought of it.

"Don't you see, Jacob? That is the attitude which draws people to you."

Jacob exhaled but said nothing.

"Look, Jacob!" continued Samuel, "to this community, you are their *tzadik*, their holy man."

Jacob actually shuddered when he heard this.

"Are you afraid of this power, Jacob?" asked Samuel.

"No," said Jacob. "Doubt picks a man's own pocket. Fear is the pain before the wound."

Silence drew its hood around both the men and pulled them closer together.

"Samuel," said Jacob, placing his hand on his friend's shoulder, "for someone to be a true *tzadik* he must wake others so they know themselves as their own *tzadik* because each of us is a reflection, a refraction of the Original Light."

Samuel pursed his lips and shook his head. "People don't have the character to live like this!"

His voice jumped with emotion. "You expect too much of them, Jacob."

Then Samuel confessed. "I'm afraid to believe this!"

"Don't be afraid to learn from fear," said Jacob. "It teaches us what we are frightened of.

"Look carefully and you will see we are all orchards hiding in seeds. You will see inside each of us is the Pharaoh. And inside every Pharaoh is a slave. And inside every slave is a Moses."

Jacob was swaying back and forth as if he were praying, his eyes shut, his voice filled with a clear cadence.

"We must lead ourselves out of the enslavements we have constructed and called Pharaoh.

"We must be the Moses in our Egypt. We must be the mountain in our desert. And . . ."

"And," Samuel interrupted, chorusing Jacob's rhythm, "we are the border we must cross over to enter the Promised Land."

"Ah," said Jacob, "see what a *tzadik* you are, Samuel."

REALITY RIDES
THE CURRENT

*T*HE children arrived after school. They folded their bodies onto the flour sacks.

A warmth reflected between the faces of the children and the child in Jacob.

The proximity to this warmth caused Jacob to reflect, "Vision is often the distance I need to see what is directly in front of me."

A boy found his courage and asked Jacob, "Why do you say, 'A child sees what I only understand' ?"

Jacob paused a moment before answering, letting the silence draw the boy's face upward.

When Jacob spoke, his voice had a long-ago quality.

"Imagine a boy, sitting on a hill, looking out through his innocence on the beauty of the world.

"Slowly, the child begins to learn. He does this by collecting small stones of knowledge, placing one on top of the other.

"Over time, his learning becomes a wall, a wall he has built in front of himself.

"Now, when he looks out, he can see his learning, but he has lost his view.

"This makes the man, who was once the boy, both proud and sad.

"The man, looking at his predicament, decides to take down the wall. But, to take down a wall also takes time, and, when he accomplishes this task, he has become an old man.

"The old man rests on the hill and looks out through his experience on the beauty of the world.

"He understands what has happened to him. He understands what he sees. But, he does not see, and will never see the world again, the way he saw it as a child on that first, clear morning."

"Yes . . . but," interjected a little girl unable to contain herself, "the old man can remember what he once saw!"

Jacob's head swiveled toward the child.

"You are right. Experience matures to memory. But memory is the gentlest of truths."

"Are you afraid of growing old, Jacob?" asked a child, giggling while she spoke.

"What grows never grows old," said Jacob.

WHAT ISN'T SAID
IS ALSO HEARD

A man and a woman came to Jacob, concerned because they could not communicate their feelings for each other and feared this expressed a void in their relationship.

Jacob listened to the couple, letting his eyes wander between their eyes.

"If you don't have words," said Jacob, "then share what you do have. Share the silence."

"But," said the woman, "how can we talk to each other in silence?"

"Ah," Jacob reminded, "isn't that why you came to see me? Because what isn't said between people is also heard!"

DEATH IS ALSO A DOOR

*T*wo children, who had become dependent on Jacob, were concerned about what they would do as he grew older and one day died.

Jacob, sensing this, drew the children near and told them this story:

"Once there was a student who was with a teacher for many years. And, when the teacher felt he was going to die, he wanted to make even his death a lesson.

"That night, the teacher took a torch, called his student, and set off with him through the forest.

"Soon they reached the middle of the woods where the teacher extinguished the torch, without explanation.

" 'What is the matter?' asked the student.

" 'This torch has gone out,' the teacher answered and walked on.

" 'But,' shouted the student, his voice plucking his fear, 'will you leave me here in the dark?'

" 'No! I will not leave you in the dark,' returned his teacher's voice from the surrounding blackness. 'I will leave you searching for the light.' "

ON THE OTHER SIDE

*J*ACOB walked next to the river.

It's path ran like a long, blue vein on the back of an ancient hand.

Crickets sang, and their song was so consistent the music ceased.

A blush of breeze rose from the grass. Jacob felt as if an angel's wing had beat against his cheek. He touched his cheek slowly. He felt embarrassed by the thought.

"That I should think an angel came to me."

He wept. And, again, the brush of breeze against his cheek.

Jacob decided he would not sleep that night. He chose instead to lie on top of the covers and trace his breathing.

By following his breath, he hoped to find the trail by which breath was given to this world.

He saw himself as a boy, sitting and dreaming on the porch of his parent's home, laying his cheek on the cement steps made warm by the spring sun.

He saw the bakery, the tracks of the pigeons, the significance of a single footprint left casually in the dust.

He saw time and the way it unwound a man.

He saw himself release thought and judgment.

He saw the shape before form, the view before the wall.

And then he stopped seeking and knowing.

And then he was at one with the One.

And there was nowhere else for him to be.

MY HEART KNOWS
WHAT MY MIND
ONLY THINKS IT KNOWS

*M*ax was chasing pigeons out of the back door of the bakery when he noticed Jacob coming toward him.

He offered Jacob a wide grin and welcome.

"Hey, Jacob! What's going on here? You going to make us all holy men?"

Jacob looked up from below the loading dock and laughed.

"No, Max. God made you holy. And, you are responsible for knowing that."

"Not me," said Max. "You're the saint!"

Jacob let the idea of this pass over him without any resistance. He reminded himself, "To deny a thought is to engage a thought."

Jacob walked into the bakery and stopped. His eyes rose and settled in a slow, arching vision of the space. He thought of how many times he had stared at the abstract shadows the sun sketched on the walls.

He wondered how many of the details in this moment among moments would cling to him when all this dissolved.

Someone touched Jacob's elbow. He returned.

It was someone he hadn't seen before.

"Are you Jacob?" she asked.

He considered that a good question.

The woman waited for an answer.

"Yes, I am Jacob."

"A few moments ago, you were standing very quietly. What were you doing?"

"I was praying," said Jacob, without a trace of self-consciousness.

"Praying for what?" asked the lady.

"Praying to be Jacob."

"That doesn't make sense!"

"Good, the reason for religion is not reason."

"What does that mean?"

"It means, I don't pray because it makes sense to pray. I pray because my life doesn't make sense without prayer."

"Ohhh," said the woman, stretching the word into several syllables.

The sunlight, which only moments before had been transporting Jacob, now passed like an oriental fan across the woman's face.

"Why did you come to see me?" asked Jacob.

The woman lowered her eyes for a moment and then ventured out again in a series of quick questions.

"People say, you believe in God. Is that true?"

"I say, God believes in us."

"Yes, but do you trust God?"

"Faith uses its strength to develop trust."

"Do you think God is a man?"

"No, but I don't think God is not a man either. I think God is."

Jacob's answers made it difficult for the woman to hold to the questions she thought were on her agenda.

"Jacob," she asked with an innocence which surprised herself, "is it hard to pray?"

"Sometimes it is difficult to get out of my own way," said Jacob.

"And what does that mean?"

Jacob's smile wrinkled warmly. "That means I am often more of a wall than a window to myself."

"So," she said, "prayer removes the obstacles in life?"

"Prayer many times brings together . . . what never was apart.

"Prayer reminds me," he said, "that I'm not lost in a dream. I'm only dreaming I am lost."

"Do you always pray in the same way, Jacob?"

Jacob spoke slowly. "Ritual gives form to passion. Passion without form consumes itself."

"The children said you told them, 'Prayer is the path where there is none.' "

Jacob's eyes drew back their last curtain. "Yes. Prayer is a path where there is none, and ritual is prayer's vehicle."

EACH OF US
IS THE SOURCE
OF THE OTHER'S RIVER

*T*HERE was a man who was married to a very wise woman. In time, the man became jealous of his wife's wisdom.

Insecure inside and angry outside, the man argued to himself that, since man was created before woman, man was clearly superior.

Seeking support for his insecurity, he sought Jacob at the bakery.

"Woman was created from the rib of man," said the husband, beginning to build a case for himself.

"Yes," said Jacob, barely looking up. "Woman was made from the rib of a man. But, from what was man created?"

"Well, from the ground, the earth, of course."

"And," said Jacob, "isn't a woman the earth which receives your seed?"

"Yes," said the man, feeling foolish.

Jacob stopped what he was doing and spoke with the ease of truth.

"Each of us is the source of the other. And our only strength is in knowing this."

MORE PATHS CROSS
THAN MEET

"*J*ACOB!" a voice demanded through the din of the bakery. "When will the Messiah come?"

Jacob turned from the dough bench and found the man behind the question.

"You know," said Jacob, "there is an old story that, if we were to treat every person we met as if they were the Messiah, then it wouldn't make any difference if they weren't."

And, while Jacob spoke, he began to wander in his own thoughts:

"If God made man by filling him with His holy breath, then God has whispered into each of us.

"So, each time we exhale, we are releasing God's breath, the message of God's being.

"That means we are all messengers from the Source, and maybe, if we treated every person we met as if they were a messenger, we would get the message!"

These thoughts calmed Jacob, but the man who asked the question had grown impatient.

"Jacob, do you sincerely think we are capable of treating everyone as if they were the Messiah?"

"I don't know," said Jacob.

The questioner seemed to enjoy the idea of this. "You don't know?"

"My friend," said Jacob, meaning it with his voice, "the furthest a wise man can travel is to the border of his ignorance. The furthest a wise man can see is to the beginning of his blind-ness."

The man threw up his arms, clearly disgusted with Jacob's answers.

"I was told you were a holy man, a prophet, a teacher, but, instead, you tell me that you don't know, that you are ignorant, and that you are blind."

Jacob patiently nodded through the negative description.

"Well," the scoffer continued, "what should I see in you?"

"A man," said Jacob, speaking slowly, "and, in reflection, you might find I look a great deal like you."

GIVING
GIVES ME
AN OPEN HAND

An older man, who was both wealthy, and suspicious, invited Jacob to dinner in order to test him.

When the dinner was served, Jacob was given an empty plate and cup while his host's plate overflowed and his cup had wine draining past its brim.

Jacob said nothing but sat there and watched the man devour his sumptuous meal.

When the man had finished, Jacob stood, said thank you for his dinner, and prepared to leave.

Unable to resist Jacob's silence, the host asked, "Weren't you angry because I gave you nothing?"

"No," said Jacob, passing through the door.
"You gave me what you had. If I expected more
from you than I received, then I was filled with
my expectation and not your offer."

ONLY THE LIVING DIE

A woman, whose father had passed away, came to see Jacob because there was a tradition to cover the mirrors during the time of mourning, and she struggled to understand the significance of this act.

"Is it so I do not concern myself with vanity but think about my father?"

"Yes," said Jacob.

"Is it so I do not see myself in this deep sadness?"

"Yes," said Jacob.

"Is it so I do not confuse the image of life with life itself?"

"Yes," said Jacob.

"And what else Jacob?"

"Well," said Jacob, "if it is death that gives life meaning, then, perhaps, this tradition is to remind us that, when we have not lost someone, we shouldn't lose ourselves by refusing to pay attention to who we are, what we have been, what we are becoming."

UNDERSTANDING IS LIVING IN A HOUSE WHERE EVERY ROOM HAS A POINT OF VIEW

A man with a glow in his eye, a man who had turned his vision into a mission, came to see Jacob.

"Jacob, I have come to invite you to take up 'the cause' with me!"

"I am only a baker," said Jacob.

"Come on, Jacob," said the man, waving his hand with contempt at the factory, "you are much more than a baker."

"Really?" asked Jacob. "How much more could I be?"

"It is written," said the man, "that we are to be a light unto the nations."

Jacob had seen this form of self-inflation many times and was clearly not comfortable with it.

"To be a light unto the nations does not mean we are to put the spotlight on ourselves. It means we must all know we are living in the dark, and it is our mutual ignorance that reminds us we are brothers and sisters."

"I see the light," asserted the man, hoping to invoke Jacob's interest.

But Jacob recognized the look in the man's eye and replied simply, ". . . good," leaving the other man to pick up his argument.

"Good?" said the man. "I tell you I see the light, and all you tell me is 'good'! You should prepare yourself to come with me."

"I can't," said Jacob.

"Why?"

"Because I do not follow a man."

The man was crestfallen. "I'm sorry you will not join me."

"But, I am with you," said Jacob. "We are all a reflection of the One Light. We are all on a journey between destinations that do not exist. We are each other. To think otherwise is a case of mistaken identity."

The man moved off slowly.

As soon as he was out of earshot, a woman poked at Jacob with her chin and asked:

"Why didn't you tell that man he was crazy?"

"Why?" asked Jacob. "Because understanding is living in a house where every room has a point of view. Sanity may be only mutually agreed upon reality and reality a handle of convenience we attach to our experience. Perhaps he saw other realities. Too often, those who do not dream seek to destroy the dreamer by waking him."

"Huh?" said the lady, unsure what Jacob meant and raising her nose. . . . "Well, he shouldn't have treated you that way."

But Jacob was not confused about who he was. "The part of that man that I did not like is also a reflection of me!"

ARRIVING AT OUR
EXPECTATIONS

A young man, caught in an argument with himself, came to see Jacob.

"I want to believe in God but I don't understand God," he said.

"Neither do I," said Jacob. "But, then, God isn't designed to fit into my mind. Each of us is from the hand of God. None of us is The Hand."

"Well, how can you have faith when you look at all the terrible things that have happened to innocent people?"

"Because there is great sadness in life does not mean God doesn't exist. I choose hope over despair."

"So you have no proof."

"Most of us find what we are looking for," said Jacob. He looked up and saw clouds circling inevitably toward rain.

"Walk with me for a while," Jacob said to the young man, and they moved silently through the changing weather.

Then, without explanation, Jacob stopped and told his companion to find a tree that they could plant.

"A tree?" asked the young man. "If we plant a tree here by the road, someone else will certainly come along and chop it down."

"Very well," said Jacob. "I will plant the tree."

"But what shall I do?" asked the young man.

"Oh, you?" asked Jacob, his mind acting as if it were already somewhere else. "You will find somebody to chop down the tree."

FROM WITHIN A DAYDREAM, I AWAKE FROM WITHIN A MOMENT, I RETURN TO TIME

THE night brought its own silence, and this silence carried its own sounds.

Jacob sat at home, sat staring at his fingers which were laced together in his lap.

In the distance, his mind crossed and re-crossed the river.

He could see the bridge like a wooden hand reversely cupped and spanning the river.

He saw every obstacle as an experience waiting for a person whose faith would bridge his doubts.

He studied notes to himself that lay in his room like the random scattering of leaves in fall.

"No act is an orphan."

"The fruit of a lie is rotten before it is ripe."

"The wealthy will throw coins over a wall to the poor but will not pay to have the wall taken down."

"The moments we do not spend are not saved."

Jacob's mind stepped out onto its bridge, listened for his doubts, and felt The Hand beneath him stir.

IN THE ASHES

*W*HEN Jacob woke, he opened his eyes cautiously.

He reassured himself by measuring his pace in each word of his morning prayer.

He was anxious to get to the bakery while it was still dark, to lay his cheek on the warming oven.

Nevertheless, halfway to the bakery, Jacob decided to stop at Mr. Gold's, hoping he would be awake.

Under the lamp post of a full moon, Jacob rapped gently on the shutters closeting Mr. Gold's window.

Mr. Gold heard the sound and thought he was a young man again, being called to prayers.

"I'm coming! I'm coming!" he shouted to the dawn.

Jacob was touched to see memory capable of drawing Mr. Gold out of the darkness.

When he saw it was Jacob, Mr. Gold motioned for his friend to come in and grew a smile for his company.

Then, just as quickly, Mr. Gold's head dipped downward. "Do you know who I am, Jacob?"

He didn't give Jacob an opportunity to speak.

"I am an old man, and I am dying."

Mr. Gold seemed to sink beneath his sadness.

"Tell me, Jacob. Is this it?" He motioned around the room. "Is there nothing more? We become attached to this life only to be torn from it like some crude joke in the stars."

"We make life not only crude but cold," said Jacob, "by dressing ourselves in a nakedness woven from our own ignorance."

Then Mr. Gold spoke again from behind his sadness. "It doesn't make sense," he said. "Our days amount to nothing!"

Jacob's eyes listened without arguing or agreeing. He thought of the pain festering in Mr. Gold's words.

When Jacob spoke, his voice unfolded with the attitude of a man not filled with knowing but caring.

"Mr. Gold, all passes, nothing stops. Our days do amount to nothing, but that is because we are not a collection. We are a process.

"The truth about the seasons is that the seasons change. While everything appears to live and die, it is only the appearance of things which lives and dies. The dead are buried. Their memory is not."

Mr. Gold's voice considered Jacob's words.

"You know, Jacob, you are wise, and I am old."

"Then you already know, Mr. Gold, that the roots of time hold both memory and promise."

"Will you remember me, Jacob?"

"I promise, one day, I will join you, Mr. Gold."

Mr. Gold's laughter sounded like a trumpet and brought light to the corners of the room.

Then the silence regained its balance, and the two men sat there, making music from the quiet between their notes.

It was Mr. Gold who counted time and eventually spoke first.

"Jacob, where do you find the strength to carry on in life?"

"Life is often heavy only because we attempt to carry it," said Jacob. "But, I do find a strength in the ashes."

"In the ashes?" asked Mr. Gold.

"Yes," said Jacob, with a confirmation that seemed to have traveled a great distance.

"You see, Mr. Gold, each of us is alone. Each of us is in the great darkness of our ignorance. And, each of us is on a journey.

"In the process of our journey, we must bend to build a fire for light, and warmth, and food.

"But when our fingers tear at the ground, hoping to find the coals of another's fire, what we often find are the ashes.

"And, in these ashes, which will not give us light or warmth, there may be sadness, but there is also testimony.

"Because these ashes tell us that somebody else has been in the night, somebody else has bent to build a fire, and somebody else has carried on.

"And that can be enough, sometimes."